Curriculum Visions

Church

Lisa Magloff

A children's sing along

Word list

Look out for these words as you go through the book. They are shown using CAPITALS.

ALTAR The main focus of worship in a church. The altar is sometimes carved from stone or made of wood. It can also be a simple table. The altar has a flat top and might have objects on it, such as a cross and a Bible.

BAPTISE/BAPTISM A ceremony where a person is sprinkled with water, or immersed in water, as a way of showing they are a Christian.

BAPTISTRY A large container for water. In some churches, adults are baptised by getting into a baptistry and putting their whole body under the water.

BIBLE The book containing the main teachings of Christianity.

CATHEDRAL The most important or mother church of a diocese.

CHALICE A cup that is used to hold wine during the Eucharist ceremony. The chalice can be plain or decorated.

CHANCEL The eastern part of a church and the place between the nave and the altar.

CHAPEL A small, or medium-sized room in a Roman Catholic or Anglican church that is used for private worship or by a small group of worshippers. A Methodist church building is also called a chapel.

CLERGY, MEMBER OF THE CLERGY A person who has been specially trained to lead worship.

CONFESSIONAL Some Christians believe that it is important to confess their sins to God while a priest listens. This is done in private, in a small room or a curtained-off area called a confessional.

CONGREGATION All the people who are worshipping at a service.

CRUCIFY/CRUCIFIXION Jesus was killed when he was nailed (at his wrists and ankles) to a large, wooden cross. This is called crucifixion.

CRYPT An underground chamber where sometimes people are buried in a church.

DIOCESE An important area for the Roman Catholic and Anglican churches. It is overseen by a bishop.

DISCIPLE One of the first 12 followers of Jesus Christ.

EUCHARIST, HOLY COMMUNION, LORD'S SUPPER, MASS A ceremony where Christians drink a small amount of wine and eat a piece of special bread in order to remember Jesus' last supper with his disciples.

FONT A large container filled with water that has been blessed. The font is usually on a stand.

JESUS CHRIST The founder of Christianity. He died in 33 AD.

NAVE The main part of the church. The nave often looks like a big hall.

ORDINATION When someone who has been training to be a priest is given permission to lead acts of worship. The ceremony is led by the bishop.

PEWS Long benches where people sit during services.

PULPIT A raised position where a person stands to give the sermon.

REMEMBRANCE/VOTIVE CANDLES Candles which are sometimes lit in order to help remember other people or people who have died.

SCREEN A large painted board or cloth used to separate different parts of the church.

SERMON Teaching or preaching during a service.

SERVICE Religious worship. A service might include prayer, songs, a sermon and readings from the Bible.

SPIRE A pointed church tower.

STAINED GLASS Coloured or painted glass.

STATIONS OF THE CROSS Many churches have 14 plaques or paintings on the wall that show 14 things that are believed to have happened to Jesus on his way to be crucified. These plaques are called the stations of the cross.

TABERNACLE (AUMBRY) The bread used in the Eucharist is sometimes kept in a special cupboard called the Tabernacle.

TOWER A tall structure. In churches the tower often has bells inside.

VIRGIN MARY The mother of Jesus Christ.

Contents

 Be considerate!

When visiting a place of worship, remember that it is sacred to believers and so be considerate to their feelings. It doesn't take a lot of effort – just attitude.

A member of a choir sings hymns

What does a church look like?

There are many different kinds of churches. Each church looks different, but they all have some things in common.

A church is a place where Christians gather together to worship God.

A church is not the only place where Christians worship, but because churches are the most common religious buildings in the United Kingdom, there is probably one very close to where you live.

▼ ① This is a church that was built in Saxon times – over a 1,000 years ago. Notice how small it is and especially how small the windows are.

▼ ② Many country churches were built during a period of time called the Middle Ages, which happened between 1,000 and 500 years ago. The oldest part of this church is on the right. An extension was built on the left in Victorian times (just over a 100 years ago).

What churches have in common

You may be familiar with your own local church, but do you know what most churches have in common? Here are some pictures of churches to help you (pictures ①, ②, ③ and ④).

Let's begin by imagining ourselves outside a church. What would we see? In most cases we would see a tall building with large windows and STAINED GLASS. All but the oldest churches on this page look like this.

Towers, spires and bells

Most churches have a TOWER, a SPIRE or simply a single bell above the roof.

Just as in other religions, in the days before people had clocks and wristwatches, the bells were rung to remind people when it was time for the SERVICE. Bells are still rung, however, as part of Christian tradition.

▲ ③ Many city churches have been built in recent years, to cater for the needs of growing numbers of city dwellers.

They have most of the same features as older churches, such as a cross and a bell tower.

▼ ④ This is a modern city church built in new suburbs. It is only a few years old.

5

A large church

A traditional large church tells us much about the way many Christian buildings are designed for prayer.

Many Christian religious buildings are built on traditional lines, so let's look more closely at the main features of this kind of building.

In the shape of a cross

Picture ① shows a typical shape for a large church. You can see that it has been built in the shape of a cross. This is because the cross is the most important symbol of Christianity.

Many churches are also built so that they point to the east. They are pointing towards the city of Jerusalem, in Israel, where Christianity began.

▼ ① The main features of a large church.

North transept

Many of the windows on this building are made of **STAINED GLASS**.

Main entrance

Chapel

▲ ② This wooden SCREEN, called a rood screen, is sometimes used to separate the NAVE from the part of the church near the ALTAR.

Towers

On the outside of this church, you can see tall towers. Some churches have spires instead of towers. They help to give importance to the building. In past times, churches used to compete to have the tallest spire or tower.

Nave

Chancel

Altar

South transept

The nave of this building is very long. There is room for a large **CONGREGATION** to sit there during worship. At the end of the nave farthest from the entrance is the chancel and the altar.

Inside the church

The largest space inside the church is called the **NAVE**. All of the arches inside this building help to support the roof. They also divide the nave into sections called aisles.

You can also see that the **CHANCEL**, the place where the choir sings, is beyond the nave. At the end of the chancel is the main **ALTAR**. The altar is always raised on a platform. This is so that people sitting in the nave look up at the altar (picture ②).

Running across the church, between the nave and the chancel is the transept. Some transepts also have an altar.

Places for private worship

Some parts of the church, often called **CHAPELS**, are used for small groups of people to worship together.

Tombs and statues

People who were important to the church, the country or the region are sometimes remembered through statues and tombs inside the church (picture ③).

▶ ③ A statue on the tomb of an important person.

Inside a church

The church is made of several parts.

When you go into a church you will see that it is really a large hall. This hall may or may not be divided into sections.

Nave

The NAVE is the main hall of a church, where the worshippers sit (picture ①). A large area is needed so that many people can worship together.

The nave may contain row after row of seats or benches (called PEWS) where people (called the CONGREGATION) can sit while they worship.

There may also be an organ, a large instrument that provides music for the service.

Near where you have entered the church there may be a FONT – a place where people are BAPTISED (see pages 12 and 13).

There will also be a high platform, called a PULPIT, where a preacher can stand while giving the SERMON (picture ②).

▼ ① The nave starts at the back of the church and goes towards the altar. The pews in the nave always face towards the altar.

▲ ② The pulpit is where the preacher stands when giving a sermon, or talk, during worship.

Chancel and altar

The entrance door for most churches is actually in the 'back' of the nave. So, when you walk inside the church, you look right along its length. You may find a SCREEN between the nave and the rest of the church. Beyond this is the chancel (picture ③), where the choir sits, and finally the altar.

▼ ③ The choir stalls are found between the nave and the altar in a part of the church called the chancel.

Weblink: www.CurriculumVisions.com/church

The altar and cross

The cross and the altar are the focus of a church.

The altar, with its cross, is the focus of the church.

The importance of the altar

The altar reminds worshippers of the table at which **JESUS CHRIST** and

his **DISCIPLES** had their last meal together before Jesus was taken away and **CRUCIFIED**.

One way you can tell that the altar is very important is that all the pews face towards the altar. This is so that everyone can see the altar.

The altar is usually raised from the floor of the church and placed behind a railing called the altar rail.

◄▼ ① During worship an altar may contain a BIBLE, a cross, candles, a cup called the CHALICE and a special bread called the EUCHARIST. These pictures show you both traditional and modern altars.

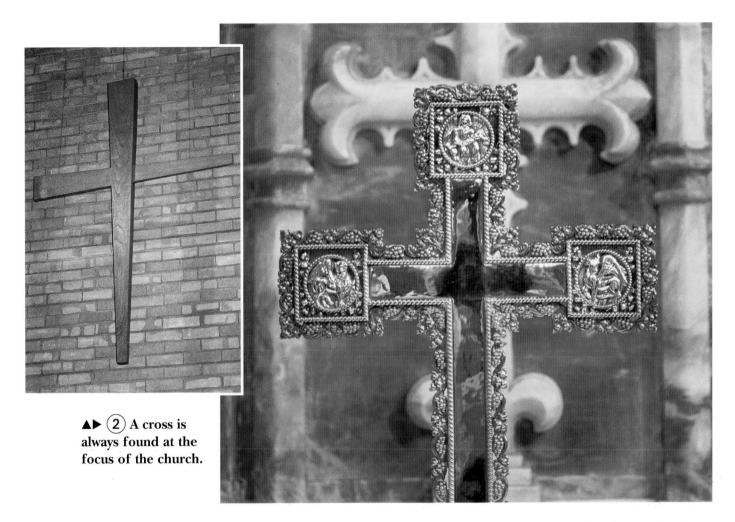

▲▶ ② A cross is always found at the focus of the church.

Behind and to the sides of the altar you may see windows, allowing the altar to be bathed in sunlight during the day (picture ①).

Behind the altar you may see a screen with paintings or carvings telling of events in the life of Jesus or the saints.

On the altar

If you were to ask people what was the most important part of a church, they would probably say the cross (picture ②).

The cross is the most important symbol of Christianity. It was on a cross that Jesus Christ died. Christians consider Him to be the sign of God.

Jesus Christ is also called the saviour.

There are many crosses in a church, but the most important one is the one that is placed on the altar. The cross and altar together make the focus for worship in a church.

There are ceremonies called the **EUCHARIST, MASS, HOLY COMMUNION** or the **LORD'S SUPPER**. During these ceremonies bread and wine are placed on the altar. This reminds worshippers of the bread and wine that Jesus shared with his disciples during their last meal. The wine is held in a special cup called the **CHALICE**.

11

Weblink: www.CurriculumVisions.com/church

To be baptised

Christians are welcomed into the Christian community by being baptised. That is why the font is such an important part of the church.

When people are **BAPTISED** they are welcomed into the church. Christian families often have their children baptised when they are babies. This is the first step on the way to being confirmed as an adult member of the Christian church.

What is the font?

The **FONT** is the part of the church where Baptism takes place (picture ①). So, the font is therefore a very important part of the church.

The font is usually in the back of the nave, near the door that people use to enter the church. The font is placed here for an important reason.

It reminds worshippers that when someone is baptised, they are entering the Christian religion.

The font can be any shape or size. Water is poured into it for the Baptism ceremony (picture ②).

Baptism as an adult

The first Christians were baptised, like Jesus, as adults. Some adults also want to be baptised. Many people feel that Baptism at this stage of life is like being born all over again. In fact, some Christians, for example, the Baptists, feel that it is important to put their whole body underwater during Baptism, and so their font is actually a small pool (picture ③). This kind of font is sometimes called a **BAPTISTRY**.

▲ ① People are baptised at the font. During Baptism, a member of the CLERGY says special blessings and then sprinkles some water from the font on to the person's head.

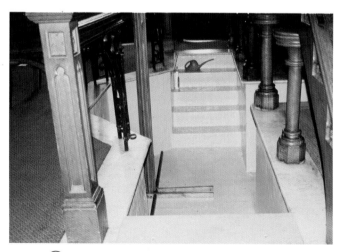

▲ ③ In some churches, people are baptised by putting their whole body underwater. In these churches, a very large font called a baptistry is used.

◄ ② A Baptism is a celebration of the official entry of a new member to the Christian faith.

Weblink: www.CurriculumVisions.com/church

Different ways to worship

Some Christians find that items such as statues, candles and the confessional help them in their worship.

There are many different Christian religious groups in the UK. Two of the main groups are the Anglicans and the Roman Catholics. They worship in a similar way but there are some differences and these affect the arrangement of a church.

For example, in a Roman Catholic church, you may see a place near an altar or a statue where there are candles alight (picture ①). These are called **REMEMBRANCE CANDLES** or Votive candles. Worshippers light these candles in order to help them pray for living people or those who have died.

Special places

In almost all Roman Catholic churches there are tiny, curtained-off areas called **CONFESSIONALS**. Worshippers use these areas to speak or confess to God while a priest listens to them.

Roman Catholic and Anglican churches have a cupboard called the

▼ ① These candles help people pray for their living friends and relatives and for those who are dead.

▲ ② Statues can also help people worship, by reminding them of important Christians and what they did. This is a statue of St Teresa of Liseaux, from a Roman Catholic church.

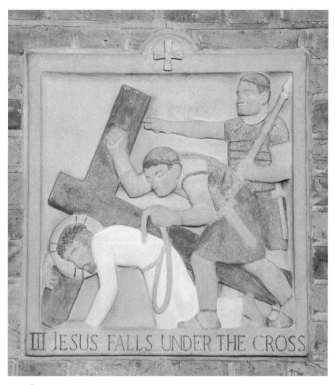

▲ ③ The stations of the cross are usually plaques or pictures that remind worshippers of 14 things that may have happened to Jesus on his way to be crucified. This is station three.

III JESUS FALLS UNDER THE CROSS

TABERNACLE. Any bread and wine that is not used in the Eucharist is kept in the Tabernacle. This bread and wine may be taken to the homes of worshippers who are ill to perform the Eucharist there.

Statues help people pray

In some Roman Catholic and Anglican churches, people like to remember important Christians when they pray. To help them, these churches might have statues or paintings of, for example, important Christians from the past (picture ②).

Many Roman Catholic churches have statues of the **VIRGIN MARY**. These statues help remind worshippers about the life of the Virgin Mary and also help them to pray.

There might also be statues or paintings near the altar, where they can be used in worship.

Special objects that help people worship

As you look around a Roman Catholic and some Anglican churches, you may see 14 plaques or paintings on the walls. These are called the **STATIONS OF THE CROSS** (picture ③).

The stations of the cross remind worshippers of fourteen things that are believed to have happened to Jesus Christ on his way to be crucified.

Plain and simple buildings

Some people find it comforting to have a ceremony and a highly decorated building. Others find it enough to meet together in a simple room.

There are many different ways for Christians to express their faith. This is why churches do not all look the same inside or outside. For example, many churches do not have tall towers outside, or statues and paintings inside. Instead they look more like ordinary buildings.

Friends Meeting House

A church does not have to be a large building or even to have a large cross on the outside. Picture ① shows a Friends Meeting House. There is no cross or **STAINED GLASS**. We know that it is a religious building because the

sign in front tells us that it is used as a religious building.

In a Friends Meeting House the members of the meeting sit on benches or chairs arranged in a square, facing each other. There is no pulpit or font, and there are no statues. There is nothing on the inside or the outside of the building to distract worshippers from thinking about God.

▼ ① This is a Friends Meeting House. You can only tell it is a religious building because of the sign at the front. The sign tells us that this is a Friends Meeting House, and tells us what time services are held.

Salvation Army Citadel

The Salvation Army Citadel is another place where people worship in plain surroundings (picture ②). However, there are more decorations than in a Friends Meeting House.

Instead of a cross, or a picture of Jesus Christ, there is a special Salvation Army emblem on the wall (picture ③).

There is no organ in a Salvation Army Citadel. Instead, there is a brass band (picture ④). The Salvation Army badge and the music of the brass band remind worshippers that they are part of God's "army".

▼ ③ Instead of a big cross, most Salvation Army churches have the Salvation Army emblem. The words "blood and fire" on the emblem remind worshippers that the church will help save them.

▼ ② The inside of a Salvation Army Citadel usually has few decorations. Worshippers sit on plain chairs and stand up to sing.

▲ ④ Most large Salvation Army Citadels have a brass band instead of an organ. The band wears a uniform. This reminds people that they are in an "army of God".

Weblink: www.CurriculumVisions.com/church

Stained glass

Many churches are decorated with stained glass windows. The windows are beautiful and the scenes in them help people worship.

When you walk into a church during the day, you might be amazed at all the beautiful colours coming from the windows. Windows like these, that are made from painted or coloured glass, are called **STAINED GLASS** windows (picture ①).

◀ ① Stained glass windows like these play a part in worship in the church. The pictures on the windows help worshippers remember important stories from the Bible.

▼ ② Some stained glass windows show saints or important local people.

Stained glass windows let light and colour into the church. Many churches have stained glass windows behind, and to the sides of the altar, so that it is bathed in colours. Some churches and **CATHEDRALS** have stained glass in almost every window.

Stained glass is very nice to look at, but it can also be helpful in worship.

Stories on windows

The stained glass windows in a church are often made so that they show scenes from the Bible or from Christian history (pictures ② and ③). The light shining through the stained glass makes the scenes look beautiful and bright.

A long time ago, when most people could not read, they would look at the stained glass windows to help them learn stories from the Bible. Today, most people can read, but stained glass windows are still used to remind people of important Christian stories and events.

▶ ③ Some churches have just a few, small, stained glass windows. But many large churches, and especially cathedrals, have stained glass in many windows. The stained glass cross in this Methodist church has pictures of the 12 disciples.

Cathedrals

A cathedral is the central or 'mother' church of an area called a diocese which is led by a bishop.

Of all the Christian buildings in the world, the ones that stand out the most are the cathedrals (pictures ① and ②).

What is a cathedral for?

The **CLERGY** in a **DIOCESE** work together. Their work is led by a bishop and a group of clergy who work at a cathedral. Important events for the city and churches of the diocese are held in the cathedral. There may be 'pop' style acts of worship or solemn ceremonies at the inauguration of a mayor and the **ORDINATION** of clergy. As in all churches there are regular services on Sundays and weekdays.

An awesome building

In the past, no money was spared to build the tallest and grandest cathedrals in honour of the glory of God. Many modern cathedrals follow the same tradition of having a large, awesome building. As a result, a cathedral is usually one of the largest and most awesome buildings in a city.

▶ ① Cathedrals like St Paul's, in London, are huge and awesome buildings.

Inside a cathedral

Just as a cathedral is built to look awesome on the outside, everything on the inside of a cathedral is also made to be huge and beautiful. For example, the nave of a cathedral might have room for thousands of people to sit (picture ③).

Inside the cathedral there might be artwork, stained glass windows (see pages 18 and 19), and a large, decorated altar and pulpit. All of these things make the cathedral a very special building.

◀ ② Westminster Cathedral is a modern Roman Catholic cathedral.

▲ ③ The choir stalls at the end of the nave in St Paul's Cathedral.

Special places inside the cathedral

A cathedral contains all the things that you find inside a church, such as the altar, font, pulpit and chapel. As in some churches, important people are buried in tombs or **CRYPTS** inside the cathedral. The tombs might be decorated with statues of the people buried there.

Cathedrals also have a special seat, called the bishop's throne. This is where the bishop of the diocese sits during worship.

Weblink: www.CurriculumVisions.com/church

Churches around the world

There are Christian religious buildings all around the world. These are often built using local materials and building styles.

Wherever people have built Christian buildings, they have often used the materials that were readily available. That is why many churches are built of stone. However, the church in picture ① is made from a kind of mud called adobe. Many buildings in desert areas of the world are made from adobe.

Different building styles

Churches also vary in shape and style from one part of the world to another. For example, in Ethiopia, Africa, some churches were carved out of rock in the shape of a cross (picture ②). By contrast, in Romania, Eastern Europe, some churches are of rounded shape and decorated with many paintings (picture ③) not just inside but also on all of the outside walls.

▼ ① **This church, in the state of New Mexico in the USA, is made of mud. That is why it has to have very thick walls. In this area rainfall is uncommon, but nevertheless, the walls have to be repaired every year or so.**

◄▲ ②An Ethiopian church in Lalibela. This church was carved out of rock and is sunk in the ground. You can see that it is in the shape of a cross.

▼ ③A Romanian church, showing paintings on the inside (left) and outside (right) of the small countryside church.

23

Index

Curriculum Visions

Curriculum Visions is a registered trademark of Atlantic Europe Publishing Company Ltd.

 Atlantic Europe Publishing

Teacher's Guide
There is a Teacher's Guide to accompany this book, available only from the publisher.

Dedicated Web Site
There's more about other great Curriculum Visions packs and a wealth of supporting information available at our dedicated web site:

www.CurriculumVisions.com

First published in 2003 by
Atlantic Europe Publishing Company Ltd
Copyright © 2003
Atlantic Europe Publishing Company Ltd
First reprint 2004

All rights reserved. No part of this publication may be reproduced, stored in a retrieval system, or transmitted in any form or by any means, electronic, mechanical, photocopying, recording or otherwise, without prior permission of the Publisher.

Authors
Lisa Magloff, BA and Brian Knapp, BSc, PhD
Religious Education Consultant
The Reverend Ian DH Robins, MA, BD, AKC
Art Director
Duncan McCrae, BSc
Editors
Barbara Bass, BA and Gillian Gatehouse
Senior Designer
Adele Humphries, BA
Acknowledgements
The publishers would like to thank the following for their help and advice:
The vicar, verger and choir of St Nicholas church, Hurst; St James Church, Muswell Hill; Our Lady of Muswell Hill; Salvation Army; Muswell Hill Baptist Church; Friends Meeting House, Muswell Hill;

the rector of Christ Church, Southborough.
Photographs
The Earthscape Editions photolibrary except page 13: *Stella Wood.*
Illustrations
David Woodroffe
Designed and produced by
Earthscape Editions
Reproduced in the Czech Republic by
Global Colour sro
Printed in China by
WKT Company Ltd

Church – *Curriculum Visions*
A CIP record for this book is available from the British Library

Paperback ISBN 1 86214 306 4
Hardback ISBN 1 86214 308 0

This product is manufactured from sustainable managed forests. For every tree cut down at least one more is planted.